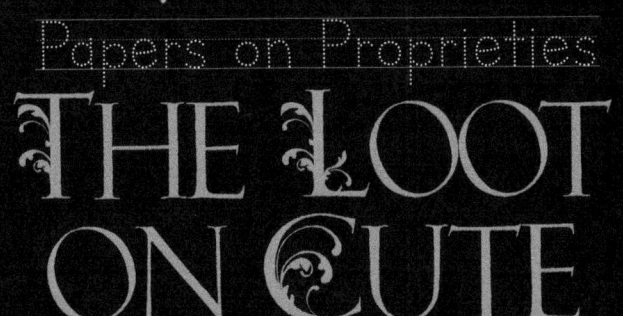

Papers on Proprieties
THE LOOT ON CUTE

NOTES FROM

23 RHUIDROCK
once upon Miss Kayt Davis' time,
The Young Ladies School
of Internal & Eternal
Beauty

Lesson 1

B. Jane Turnquest

The Loot on Cute
Papers on Proprieties

B. Jane Turnquest is a writer of books for children and adults, she also pens songs for her personal cathartic ministry. She lives in The Bahamas - to find out more about what she is writing, follow her on Facebook at B.Jane Turnquest Children's Book and Facebook & Instagram at Quill Ink Parchment Publish.

Children's books by B. Jane Turnquest

The Memoir That Makes You Go Mmm

The Contrite Contrary Chronicles

Sir Caerwyn The Knight and the
Midnight Colored Plight

Caerwyn and The Heart of The Sea

No part of this book may be reproduced in any form or by any electronic or mechanical means, including information storage and retrieval systems, without permission in writing from the publisher, except by reviewers, who may quote brief passages in a review. Scanning, uploading, and electronic distribution of this book or the facilitation of the same without the permission of the publisher is prohibited.

Please purchase only authorized electronic editions, and do not participate in or encourage electronic piracy of copyrighted materials. Your support of the author's rights is appreciated.

Any member of educational institutions wishing to photocopy part or all of the work for classroom use or anthology should send inquires to info@quillinkparchment.com

Our books may be purchased in bulk for promotional, educational, or business use. Please contact your local bookseller or Quill Ink & Parchment Publication at email info@quillinkparchment.com

Copyright© 2021 B. Jane Turnquest
All rights reserved.

Quill Ink & Parchment

PUBLICATIONS

23 Rhuidrock Towers, Nassau, Bahamas SP 60276

www.quillinkparchment.com

For

Kayt, Klaire-Destiny, Dainne, Amelia, Gwynn CC, Sy'rai, Azaliah, Saige, Jere Miah, Verni, Brianna, Breshae, Alexia, Ameera, Arianna, Vonia, Jacila R. Carle, Khyla, Jaylyn, Krimson, D'Avah, Sarai, Johniqua, Rose, Kimya, Marlee, Mila, and all the girls on my son's path in this life {for obvious reasons}.

True beauty resides
some place deep; it is found on the inside.
It spills out
through eyes, smiles, hands, and mouths.
Other words for beauty you will find,
are in the family of friendly, fair, upright,
giving, helpful, and kind.

Loveliness is not found in young ladies' varied
textures, shapes, sizes, or hues.
It is where the heart meets the mind and wills,
to do's.

The product of this benevolence gets its due,
and that is the veritable beauty that shines
through and true.

It is not about life being perfected, but how
noble pursuits outweigh, and that manners
are not neglected.

1

The first thing about beauty, to be schooled

is the truth of all truths concerning your most

precious jewel;

it is inviting, sweet, and warm;

that is the simple upturn that lips can easily form.

2

Petty is short an R;

without it, your pretty cannot go far.

Do not mix mean with minor matters.

If you do and look in the mirror, there will

be a crack or quite possibly a "complete shatter."

3

Making fun of someone for a laugh,

will assuredly decrease your charm stock by

half.

If you wish, do the teasing;

be warned;

you will end up with a look that is quite

unpleasing.

The title of queen,

will go to one using shaming, humiliating words

and acts to demean,

for the one who is a contestant in a pageant

with a mix of monstrous evils and fiends.

Measure what you do and say.

Do not allow the potency of poor words to

be the reason to ruin anyone's day.

6

Uncouth is among the chief uproot,

listed in the top three lootings of the cute.

Lacking manners, refinement, and grace?

It would not help you hold on to any beauty,

even if you had Venus' face.

7

Low in virtue and morals,

will get you accepted into the School of

the Deplorables.

8

Dear say,

do not be the one to spread hearsays

or even partake in gossip or slander.

It indeed will diminish your finish, your grandeur.

Mathematically speaking, sour + dour + glower

does not equate to a flower.

Eliminate the scowl, pout, frown, and glare,

if you want to be counted as fair.

A face that is uppity and proud,

changes the atmosphere for those you surround;

and in front of your beauty, there will also be a cloud.

Employ basic physics and note that as one turns up

a nose,

a kind smile will not, cannot exist, nor be exposed.

Always the nag or a complainer is tiresome;

it masks a face with features that is gloomy

and glum.

You will find that people, concerning you,

will always move away from.

12

A Negative Nelly, with never-ending no's and nopes,

takes your appeal out of everyone's scope.

A notorious naysayer

summons a beauty slayer.

Indulge in a negative charge,

and beware that the hope of any positive bearing

cannot materialize, or be enlarged.

Being disagreeable and contrary

will get you mirrored unsmiling faces, as you make

others weary.

13

Not answering someone and pretending to be mute,

is disrespectfully discourteous - a double dose

of don't - and the side effects are unequivocally

uncouth, and un·cute.

Always the damsel in distress; beauty-wise, it subtractive.

Attempt to be your own champion, think towards the solution, or be problem-solving combative (or at least active).

The world will find this both commendable and attractive

A lack of gratitude

affects more than your attitude.

16

Do not be a judge, and measure others or compare.

Your charm will go elsewhere.

It is distasteful and an insult.

By the way, elsewhere could be in a deep dark vault.

Mistakes happen.

Accept them and let them sharpen.

Take responsibility and do not toss the blame,

that would be a tasteless cast and poor thing

to proclaim.

18

It is beastly to berate or be the one who bullied.

Never has a bully's looks remained unsullied.

Others affair and private business,

are not yours to repeat, even if you were a

witness.

Be a blabbermouth,

and your countenance will lose its appeal,

charm, and jointly, its clout;

If you do not know how to, on occasion serve,

it will be a kind of splendor, illuminated and

magnificent, that others will never be blessed to

observe.

Learn to give back,

whether it's time or things, your appeal would

not lack.

21

When you decline, be polite.

Avoid your charm taking flight.

Do not scoff and snub.

Do you know what happens when you take

an eraser and rub?

22

When time calls for hard honesties,

use gentle words and modesties.

Put the hard words in the middle, and start

and end with kindness.

Avoid hurting others and likewise, your fineness.

Do not be known to be too thrilled,

with flashy finds, fripperies, and excess frills.

When vanity over-fills,

genuine beauty goes to the opposite and is

left near nil.

Find out others' emotional states,

before you mention the grievances on your plate.

Tactfulness and thoughtfulness make timeless

beauties, which are more than mere 'cuties.

25

Do not allow others' foulness to change you,

remain unmoved and aloof,

or risk your bearings going poof.

Have control,

or your looks will take a toll.

Be unruffled and steadfast;

your charm will last;

Toot your own horn,

looks will instantly be withdrawn.

Let your self-affirmations be uttered privately

or thought of in the mind.

Any other way, hints of superiority, which

dulls a shine.

You certainly can put your merits on display;

it is just unbecoming to publically self-praise

and say.

Don't risk being known as a boast and a brag,

and have a certainty follow, which is, your

beauty being harmed and lagged.

Hone it. Own it;

just do not broadcast with a tune to it.

A few foul F's to circumvent,

to avoid your appeal's descent.

Flighty, feckless, fickle, flagrant, fanatical

fastidious, foolhardy, featherbrain, faux,

and farcical.

29

Green is the color of envy and the shade you would be painted.

Needless to say, it seeps in and the heart ends up tainted.

Do not monopolize a conversation; allow a fair exchange.

Do not talk solely of your interests, delights, troubles, and campaigns.

The art of proper conversation allows for others to engage.

It is not polite - a monologue upstage.

Asking, telling, and listening should be a proper conversationalist's balanced attempt,

so, as not to look unflatteringly self-absorbed and be the recipient of contempt.

Make great effort not to be overbearing,

as it is at the opposing view of endearing.

Ponder the admiration, value, the heightened appeal·the mystery of a wrapped gift because its treasure is ᒼconcealed.

Have steel and grit.

Being over-sensitive, spineless, and skittish,

is never a complementing fit;

Though it should be cliché,

familiarity breeding contempt remains touché.

Not being the subject of constant talks earns one

the uncommon's fate,

like precious and rare stones, valued at the

highest rate.

35

Too much on a display mount,

due to exposure, warrants a drop in the tag,

a discount.

Have matters reserved,

for an incline of your overall curve.

Branded as a fabulist, embellisher, or a liar,

all hope of beauty will go to the pits, devastated

and dire.

Pungent scents, causing others not wanting to breathe,

will indeed be the cause for your entire look to recede.

Be well-groomed.

Look like a flower in bloom.

Boisterous, overwhelming, and crass, you will be deprived of beauty that is joined with class.

Nags,

bring to mind, hags.

Entitlement thinking,

is uninviting, and quite radiant-shrinking.

42

LB is for pounds.

Weigh these, and note, an appeal will not abound.

Lazy, lollygag, languorous, lethargic, lackadaisical,

and lackluster, are big, bold beauty busters.

Boundless bemoaning and complaining,

are all-things-pleasant draining.

If you are afforded power over others, remember abuse, oppression, and unfairness will result in your total appeal being smothered.

A sycophant is a self-seeking flatterer who aims to further their position and expand; the flip side of this is, they are disingenuous repugnant, superficial, often see-through, and bland.

46

To deride, belittle, or put others down,

will not make you look regal and imposing,

but unworthy of grace's 'crown.

An unoriginal, a copycat, a counterfeit,

produces only beauty that is illegit.

Being a sore loser, making bad exits or without merit, crying foul or cheat,

with a glance in the mirror, you will see the loss, the true defeat.

Slang is something you have to know

when and how to drop,

to avoid your refinement being filed a

fail and a flop.

Do not be the ludicrous,

if you want to reach a state of pulchritudinous.

You can have a playful or an amusing heart,

but be pleasant and respectful and, be known

for these parts.

Remember to always make a good exit.

To your reputation, this will be a credit.

BIBLE QUOTE
On What is Worthy

"Finally, brethren,

whatsoever things are true,

whatsoever things are honest,

whatsoever things are just,

whatsoever things are pure,

whatsoever things are lovely,

whatsoever things are of good report;

if there be any virtue,

and if there be any praise,

think on these things."

Philippians 4:8, KJV:

Tea Party Ideas

Themes

The Toast of The Town
Peaches & Cream
Friends in Frocks
Girls in the Garden
Manners and Maidens in the Midst
Prim Proper Pulchritudinous
Society of Girls Who Know How
Fluer Soiree
Sugar & Spice & All Things Nice
Belles of Beatitude
Queens of Pristine
Fair Hearts of the Round Table
No Bashing at the Bash
High Tea with the High-minded
Fete for the Fitting
Frolic and Fancy
Color Me Considerate

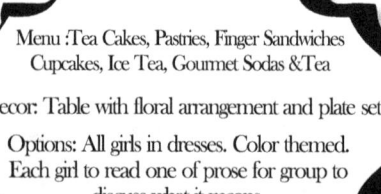

Menu: Tea Cakes, Pastries, Finger Sandwiches
Cupcakes, Ice Tea, Gourmet Sodas & Tea

Decor: Table with floral arrangement and plate set

Options: All girls in dresses. Color themed. Each girl to read one of prose for group to discuss what it means.

THE PULCHRITUDINOUS SOCIETY

CERTIFICATE

We hereby certify that

_____

has successfully completed the papers on proprieties tutorial course on

THE LOOT ON CUTE

_____
Date

B. Jane Turquest
23 Rhudrock Estates
Finishing School For Girls

The rich little poor girl caught the interest of a royal admirer, a priest, a mogul and a savant; and she refused them all. In classic fairytale fashion, she married an upstanding, handsome, clever and brave third son, and bore a son called Love Fair Blessed Famous Ruler. Overlooking the sparkling aquamarine Bahama sea, they are living amply ever after.

I would be most thankful if you enjoyed this book, and left a review on Amazon and, or Goodreads.

xoxo

www.ingramcontent.com/pod-product-compliance
Lightning Source LLC
Chambersburg PA
CBHW071857160426
43105CB00003B/1087